FURUSATO

FURUSATO

Poems by

Michael Cantor

Cover design by Shay Culligan

Cover art by Valori Herzlich

ISBN: 978-1-950462-12-4

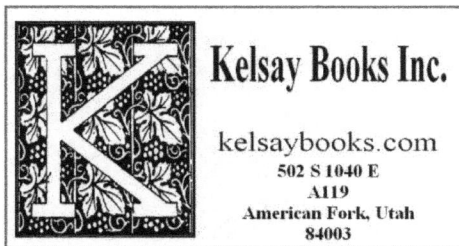

Kelsay Books Inc.

kelsaybooks.com
502 S 1040 E
A119
American Fork, Utah
84003

For my mother

Acknowledgments

Edge City Review: "1001 Ovillejos"
American Arts Quarterly: "Painted Women"
New Walk: "Furusato"
Shit Creek Review: "Lament"
Verse Wisconsin: "A Sestina for Bernie Madoff"
Cumberland Poetry Review: "Poem *Noir*"
Angle: "Summer Employment on Plover Island," "Waiting Room," "Constructionism"
Soundzine: "Is Good Life," "Sushi Sue"
New Verse News: "Candidate," "Flag Day," "The Elders"
The Performer: "Toy Soldiers"
Manzanita Quarterly: "August, 1965"
Lucid Rhythms: "To an Old Friend Who Died Young"
Muddy River: "Perdu"
Measure: "Tina," "Biographical Note"
Per Contra: "A Portrait of Dorian Greigh"
Light Quarterly: "Noblesse Oblige," "The Gallery Opening"
Iambs and Trochees: "Above Fat Papa's Bar in Casablanca"
Candelabrum: "A Bouquet of Triolets" (a portion)
14 by 14: "Tree Swallows in August"
Kin: "Rothko"
String Poet: "Refractions"
Frostwriting: "Clever," "*Querencia,*" "*Harusami,*" "A Memorial Service for my Mother, Age 102"
Autumn Sky: "The Sculptor, Dead at Age 34, and her College Admirer"
Alabama Literary Review: "Havana"
Frogpond: "Haibun: Plover Island"
Amsterdam Quarterly: "Christmas Morning at the Pueblo"
Chimaera: "At Plover Island, 9/28/01"

I wish to extend my deep gratitude to the many friends and colleagues in the Powow River Poets of Newburyport, MA, and the *Eratosphere* online poetry site, with whom I have workshopped and traded advice and poems and opinions and gossip and recipes and whatever-else-was-possible for over fifteen years, for bringing me into their community of poets, and providing the support and encouragement that helped enable this book and others. I don't think there is a poem in this collection that I have not waved before both groups, and profited from the feedback I received. I would like to list you all by name, but there are simply too many, and I don't want to overlook anybody. My thanks to all.

Contents

III. The *Tummler*

IV. At Plover Island

I.

Querencia

Biographical Note:

I am a semi-colon kind of guy;
enamored of the curlicue, the dot;
the quiet, understated way it's got
of letting life just slide and sidle by;
a ritualistic pause that may imply
a thing or two; a shrug, a sigh, is what
I choose to offer; not the cold-and-hot
assaults of passion that transmogrify

a subtle hint into a joust with God:
no images, no metaphors, no blood;
no wild-eyed horses dying in the mud;
I don't make love or war, I simply nod;
and as I semi-smile and semi-bow,
my semi-colon arcs a jaded brow.

Furusato

A Japanese Division Chief and I
are perched above the ruins of the Bronx;
our rented Town Car trapped on the Expressway,
elevated, air-conditioned, motionless;
and Mr. Kondo stares through the window
at burned-out tenements and savaged streets.
Figures scrabble through the rubble, hunting copper.
There must be an accident. Or construction.
What happened? Shit happens. *Shikata ga nai,*
the Japanese will say, "It can't be helped."
"I'm sorry for the dead at Hiroshima,"
the Emperor said, in '75,
at the first press conference he ever held,
"but there was a war. It could not be helped."
Shikata ga nai. Shikata ga nai,
we shrug and mutter tonelessly.

This should have been a clean shot to the City,
a city boy's display of city skills—
the Merritt from the factory in Connecticut,
the Hutchinson, the Bruckner, then the fun—
the secret turns, the side streets to the Willis Bridge,
the switch to Lex to dodge the crowded Drive—
then slide a quick block right on Ninety-Sixth,
and roll down glorious Park Avenue
to the Waldorf and its ranks of Japanese.

But something has gone massively awry—
has Godzilla surfaced in the East River,
sweeping Fords and Chevys off the bridges?
We fester in stalled traffic on the Bruckner.
as my passenger frowns at the South Bronx,

at blocks and blocks of boarded-up windows,
at the bold "X"s painted on raw plywood,
and makes involuntary sucking noises.
I wonder what it is that triggers me
even as I lean in, poke at Mr. Kondo,
and make a sweeping gesture at the landscape:
Watakushi no furusato desu.
"This is my *furusato.* My home town."
Furusato! That loaded, ancient word.
This is where my people lived, the place
that we are from; my ancestors lie here,
 is what it says when said in Japanese.
The sucked-air sound was louder now.

> *"You don't need me," a Tokyo attorney said*
> *about the purchase of a factory site.*
> *New Hampshire-born, he'd made Japan his home.*
> *"You don't need me," he said with Yankee truth,*
> *"and neither do you need a title search.*
> *The Japanese have been right here forever.*
> *They didn't steal their land from the Indians,*
> *everything's recorded in the register,*
> *and everybody knows where everybody's from."*

I could have said to Kondo-san that I was raised
not far from here, but in another world.
On Yom Kippur my father stood outside the shul,
and shnored the tickets he could not afford.
The three Walsh girls wore thick plaid skirts,
I heard the middle one became a nun.
But *furusato* is where life begins,
and today life started on the Bruckner Elevated

17

trapped in the motionless afternoon traffic,
looking at block after block after block of decay,
and waiting for Godzilla to emerge.

Furusato, Mr. Kondo echoed,
gazing sideways at me, and then the Bronx,
and, almost imperceptibly, he bowed,
and bowing, sitting, slid an inch away.

The Love of Sushi Sue

I lived near Tokyo's Hama-Zushi bar
those years I was a seafood sybarite—
would start off there with monkfish caviar
and sweet live shrimp, to set the appetite—
then grab a cab to narrow streets where night
rolled into dawn, and hunt for something more.
I'd often wander home about first light
to find Old Hama, sweeping out his store.
He'd eye the catch that wiggled past his door,
but knew my true love was an artful blow
fish broth, or chunks of fatty tuna, raw,
caressed with strands of gleaming herring roe.
Good food was all I worshipped and revered
and women, though amusing, interfered.

In time, the real-life girlfriends disappeared,
replaced by fantasies of Sushi Sue
who, naked as a salmon, commandeered
my reveries—slim sushi ingenue
enshrined behind Old Hama's bleached bamboo.
She worked like nude quicksilver, with a blade
in each small hand—Hama's fish swam through
her fingers and in seconds were fileted,
embraced by rice and seaweed, and arrayed
with fat carp's heads and pouting silver bream—
sea urchin eggs, fresh squid and trout—displayed
as backdrop for my slick, wet ocean dream.
But Sue repelled me when I cupped her breast:
A sushi girl cannot make love to guest!

Although all that was years ago, the quest
remains. My thoughts have never wandered far
from Hama's pickled prawns with lemon zest,
the earthy taste of slow-baked arctic char—
or Sushi Sue's small room behind the bar—
where I now nibble her *hirame,* coax
the sweetness from her *uni,* feel a star
ignite within me as she lightly strokes
my *ana-kyu,* and whispers private jokes.
The night moves on from sake sips to nips
and licks of salty flesh whose taste evokes
a sigh—and *mirugai*—from parted lips.
"I'm glad that you like raw fish," she will coo,
as I finally taste the love of Sushi Sue.

Notes:

hirame: Halibut. Often served as a sashimi style first course, with a *ponzu* dipping sauce (lime juice, soy sauce and sake).

uni: Sea urchin gonads.

ana-kyu: A conical, hand-made sushi specialty of rice, cucumber strips and grilled ocean eel, topped with a thick, sweet sauce and rolled in seaweed. They are almost impossible to eat without dripping the impenetrable sauce on your wrist, and devotees wear these stains as badges of honor, like the nicotine-drenched fingers of post-war French intellectuals.

mirugai: A large clam. Analogous to a New England quahog.

Tokyo: 1963/2013

Deru kugi wa utareru—
"The nail that sticks out will be hammered down,"
the saying went, as everybody knew:
Deru kugi wa utareru—
observe, agree, conform, abide; be true
to what you're told, obey without a frown.
Deru kugi wa utareru—
"The nail that sticks out will be hammered down."

But that was long ago, and this is now,
and surely no one thinks that way today,
or trains employees on the proper bow,
for that was long ago, and now is now,
and what is very different now is how
businessmen have learned to smile and say
that that was long ago, and this is now,
and surely no one thinks that way today.

August, 1965

The smallest and youngest came first
We could hear them before we could see them
A kilometer down from the grandstand
Out of sight past a rise in the road

We could hear them before we could see them
A kingdom of crickets was chirping
Out of sight past a rise in the road
The children were marching and chanting

A kingdom of crickets was chirping
We still could not quite understand them
The children were marching and chanting
We waited, like crows on a fence

We still could not quite understand them
The twentieth year since the sun burst
We waited, like crows on a fence
The marchers now almost upon us

The twentieth year since the sun burst
They have emptied the country of children
The marchers now almost upon us
Holding pennants and banners and chanting

They have emptied the country of children
Fifty thousand here marching this morning
Holding pennants and banners and chanting
"No more Hiroshima, no more…"

Fifty thousand here marching this morning
Through twisted and savaged gray concrete
"No more Hiroshima, no more…"
"No more Nagasaki, no more…"

22

Through twisted and savaged gray concrete
A kilometer down from the grandstand
"No more Nagasaki, no more…"
The smallest and youngest came first.

Harusami

(a quintanka)

Now the hiss of rain
on the path we used to walk.
 Nothing has been missed.
 Maids whisper in the twilight,
 planning for the snack ahead.

Enoki, carp's head,
harusami noodles light
as silken spring rain.
In the courtyard evening mist
settles on a gravel walk.

It is good to walk
again through dark stone and mist
touching head-on-head.
A small bridge and slants of rain
flicker in the lantern's light.

Patterns on a light
yukata enlace the rain.
Fingers slowly walk
from bare neck to face to head
tracing all that has been missed.

The inn wraps in mist.
An unblinking Buddha's head
and a single light
guard the garden and the walk.
We embrace the sound of rain.

A walk in the rain,
a man, a woman, light mist:
pines twist overhead.

Note:

The *quintanka* form, which is my invention, consists of five related tanka stanzas. As in a sestina, the end words are the same in each stanza, but the order changes. There is also a three line haiku envoi, which uses all five words.

Haibun: Divorce

late night temple bell
her hands like spring raindrops
on my naked back

quiet ryokan
the cormorants at Gifu
this woman and I

The divorce is sophisticated and civilized, very New York, and we
are proud of ourselves. Friendly and amicable. No kids. She gets
custody of the Lhasas. I have already started referring to them as
my ex-dogs. I have most of the Imari ware, and the Hamada Shoji
bowl we found in Kyoto. People grow. Sachiko drew and painted, I
returned frequently to Japan on business, and found other women
who were attracted to men who read books in bars. Then I came
home and counted her finished canvases, and estimated how much
work had been done, and rolled my bathrobe sleeves back down,
and threw out the tissues or cigarettes—a lipstick, once—I
sometimes found in the pockets. "You fucked another woman, or a
dwarf," I said. Sachiko went for a long run in the Park. We saw a
revival of *A Touch of Class* at the Modern a few years ago, with
Glenda Jackson and George Segal as the terribly cool London
lovers, and there was a lovely line about always being faithful as
long as they were in the same country at the same time, and
everybody laughed but us.

from her living room
we watch the cabs on Lexington
an ex-wife and I

Yojimbo

A puppy trots up with a severed hand,
and Kurosawa knew what not to say:
a wordless image makes you understand.
The camera lingers on a burning sleigh.

It was a time of films and sex and play.
A puppy carries in a dead man's hand.
At Marienbad we idolized Resnais,
and spent our youth in an exalted land.

Enraptured with ourselves, involved and grand,
there were no thoughts about the end of day.
A puppy's playing with a severed hand.
You wore blue. The Germans were in gray.

These memories are now in disarray,
and films, and life, turned difficult yet bland:
it's time to step away from vérité.
A puppy enters with a dead man's hand.

A View of Mount Fuji

There are two types of fools the proverb cites:
Those who have never scaled Mt. Fuji's heights—
climbed through the night to see the rising sun
declare the day resplendently begun—
and others, who come back and do it twice.

He heard the words and wished at once to try,
to rise to stand where sacred place meets sky;
and knew, with inner pride, he'd be the kind
to do it *twice*—the type the Gods assigned
to be the fool whom others glorify.

But each July as climbing season came
the weeklies and the papers would proclaim:
TEN THOUSAND HIKE UP FUJI-SAN TODAY
with shots of mobs of school kids on their way
and worker's clubs, and old folks, and the lame.

And he remained at home each year, and never
joined that crowd; nor let himself endeavor
other peaks, or try and fail, or choose,
one time, to chance a loss of face and lose:
avoided looking like a fool. Forever.

The Fall of Paris

In November of that year, the Japanese
women entered Paris. They wore long, dark
skirts of a soft fabric that clung to the outlines
of their thighs and worked well around the hips,
and hooded tops in muted colors. A female ninja
army camped each night in small hotels surrounding
the Etoile, and flowed mornings down the boulevards
and across the bridges, and invaded Rue Jacob and Rue
des Beaux Arts, and buckled gallery windows on Rue Dragon
with the power of its perfect skin.

By early spring the boutiques on
the farther side had capitulated. Moss green banners with gold
calligraphy danced on the Quai d'Orsay, and the French
retreated to enclaves bordering the Bois de Boulogne.
When fraternization began, collaborators swore the
small bodies of the visitors were virtually hairless.
A witticism passed around, based on knowing
that the Japanese word for nose, *hana,* is
pronounced in French as *ana*, which in
Japanese means "hole". Life went on.

The Disappearance

There were no kids, the dogs are dead, and we're
completely out of touch. Old friends lived near,
and now or then I'd get a call and hear
that one had seen her, sitting in the rear
at some designer's show, or sipping kir
with groups of those young men who just appear
at every function, slim and cavalier,
and that she still looked good—but slightly queer,
and was not aging well—and I would fear
that she had asked for me. But year by year
my thoughts and interests moved from there to here.
The friends are gone—no longer volunteer
small updates on her sightings. Would a tear
or two in private now be real—or insincere?

Perdu

We smoked Gauloises
in Antwerp
and drove South weekends
Sat in the Deux Magots
squinting
held the cigarettes just so
emulating Him and Her

Late at night
early in the morning
upstairs in the Hotel Bonaparte
we'd make love and make love and make love
with the windows open
hear the scrapes of chairs
the conversations from the street
smell chestnuts
flowers and each other

Or maybe it was Gitanes
and Café Flore
perhaps we were just friends
I spent an afternoon at book stalls
while she was with a married boyfriend
Who can remember the details
so long ago

but we were there
and looked at the girls in the streets
their sweater sleeves rolled down and long
good French legs
and a way of holding the head

a bit off to the side
small heads
everything angled
everything croissants dipped in strong coffee
Pernod with water

Noblesse Oblige

My gracious Brussels host in '63
was long-nosed Guy—de Bakker Delacroix.
Unschooled, I did not realize that he
was distantly related to the *roi,*
or that, in Belgian names, the small *"d" "de"*
bespoke a landed *haute* nobility
which nurtured ties to common folk as the
pluperfect sense of aristocracy.

No one explained to me the reason why
Guy asked if I would join a family dance,
or that his youngest sister's silken thigh
thrust sweetly through my legs, as if by chance,
was just her way of waltzing, not a call
to flee big brother's stuffy Christmas ball.

My mother never thought to teach me that
when strolling darkened, portrait-covered walls
it's best to say, *Strong jaw. Fine sword. Nice hat!*
Is that an early Rembrandt, or a Hals?
Not, *Voulez-vous permettez-moi?* and leer
and grab, and cruelly trip into a pair
of spindly chairs inlaid with aged veneer.
I only wish I had been more aware.

I've lived in Belgium now, and I've learned this:
if cloistered beauties seem to beg a siege,
and show a glowing, anxious cheek to kiss—
be sure it's more than mere *noblesse oblige.*
And keep in mind—it is so apropos—
that in the Belgian language, *"non"* means "no".

Havana

From the photographs of Robert Polidori

This door may once have been a shade of blue,
imbued with green, perhaps, to match the sea;
the shattered walls show hints of apricot,
on swaths of plaster of some unknown hue.
Mistress of these heat-and-salt-air-sodden rooms
where paint has lost the will to cling to paint,
Senora Luisa Faxas sits
in front of her piano and bookshelves and art;
where drunken chandeliers and mirrors dangle,
irriguous and decadent and lush,
angled in the ruins of beams and laths.

Who is Senora Faxas, who was she
with her fifteen foot ceilings and marble floors,
and ballrooms flowing endlessly to other rooms?
Has she read the piles and piles of books
stacked on floors and desks, eroded, melted,
recongealed into blocks of ink and pulp?
Did she bring back the gilded frames and massive
canvases of nudes from trips to Paris and Milan?

And what of the Condessa de Buenavista?
Is she accommodating boarders now?
Antonio Machado Ponce de Leon,
white-haired, handsome, with a dueler's scar,
has a daybed in her tortured drawing room,
walled off by hanging cotton sheets.
And Jose Ortiz Arabella lounges
shirtless, cautious, on a mold-stained couch.
Or are these lovers, cousins, serving men?

There are no answers, only photographs.
A fifties Chevrolet has gone to ground;
two-tone-hard-top-blistered-red-white beast,
the mouth and trunk agape, propped up on crates;
it decorates a side street, soundlessly.
All clocks have stopped, the clouds of birds are gone,
the walkers on the empty Boulevards,
the watchers leaning on their windowsills
are blank and motionless, figures on a scrim
that will no longer roll. A gray sea pounds
unceasingly against the Malecon.

Christmas Morning at the Pueblo

This handsome Navajo
who stood and watched the line of dancers
Christmas morning at the Pueblo
was slim and straight as Gary Cooper—
jet hair pulled back
and gathered with a silver clip,
black burnished boots of buttered elk,
black well-cut pants, black shirt, a camel
coat draped loosely on his shoulders.
He did not gossip with the pairs
of tribal cops in stained gray uniforms,
or smile at the roaming teen-age girls,
did not fit with this Christmas scene.
We named him Cashmere Overcoat.

He deals raw cocaine, she said,
in from LA to visit mom.
Or maybe he's a Stanford grad,
an MBA and poker pro.

This scene was no Nativity:
we were in a *Pueblo;* crumbly,
dun adobe buildings and some single-wides,
out on a mesa south of Taos;
earth, wind, dust, papers,
cigarette wrappers swirling in the grassless square,
broken chairs in front of houses,
two backboards and two crooked hoops.

And Cashmere Overcoat,
who looked right past the tribal elders;
old men with flat haircuts
and VFW faces, zipper jackets,
two in wheelchairs,

centered in a spot of honor
in the dirt courtyard.
He ignored the yipping dogs
and the crazy man on crutches
and the torn magazines blowing between houses
and the junked cars
and the smell of fried bread and coffee,
and even the Anglo tourists,
there to see the dancers
Christmas day at 1:00 PM,
listed in *What's Happening in Santa Fe.*

Coke and meth and crank, I said.
He's Al Pacino's secret twin—
but, better yet—an orthodontist!
His name is really Silver Braces.

The file of drums and flutes and dancers
kept snaking from a meeting hall,
the older men in front, traditional,
turquoise, silver, buckskin, moccasins,
full feathered headdresses on three or four;
stamping down their legginged feet,
setting up a beat,
and followed by a string of young and old
in every possible attire,
all intimately focused on the sound,
the beating and the rhythm,
and the ground;
precisely navigating every step,
the chanting, and the clap.

I saw him in a film, she said.
He played the Chief, the handsome one
who loved the Colonel's daughter.

As they came around a second time,
Cashmere Overcoat
meticulously folded up the coat,
placed it on a sprung-back chair
and asked some women there to watch it for him;
spoke briefly to an elder in a leather vest,
then slid into a space that opened in the line between
a thick and buffalo-looking man,
and a teen in Keds, a sweatshirt and torn jeans.
Staring tightly at the ground he moved
into the music, danced, expressionless,
his boots in cadence with the beat,
the black pants quickly filmed with dust.

Querencia

Querer: *to want, desire, wish for, love.*
Words mean only what we want them to.
There are no certain meanings, only context.
Context sends the message, context rules.

Find your security within the walls
of La Querencia, the brochure states.
At seven thousand feet in Santa Fe
the air is thin, the winter sun still strong;
as shadows lengthen, tones intensify.
Chamisa straggles down the dry arroyo
in puffs of black and gray; silver junipers
scrabble after water in the clay.

Querencia: *a place where one feels safe;*
a comfort zone, a favorite site, a haunt.
Kabuki colors—gray, black, muted greens,
deep brown and gold—commingle with Southwestern
shades of tan; and here are Hokusai prints,
assemblages of kiln-fired earthenware,
good tribal rugs, and shelves and shelves of books.

At rest, retired, tired, gone to ground,
we keep the kiva flames at La Querencia.
Twisted, bare piñones mark the sky
like brush marks on a *kakemono* scroll.
Querencia: *where one feels most at home;*
the place from which we speak our deep beliefs;
a place in which we know just who we are.

At Plaza Mexico *aficionados* pissed
in empty beer containers; gravely lobbed them
at the *ricos* in the good seats far below.
Aztec rain, you assholes. Go with God.
A wounded bull retreats to his querencia,
that spot within the ring where he feels safe;
his patch of sun-baked sand, his home, his stand.
And bows his head, and stains the ground, and dies.

Memories of Oso

From her rooftop we can see the city
swirl and flow around us in this pretty
district where the streets are named for rivers—
Tiber, Ebro, Rio Rhin, Guadalquivir.

Oso never sweats when we make love,
or lie for hours in the terrace sun;
her silken body seems to have no glands,
the skin displays no flaws, no scars or bruises,
no spots of roughness at the knees and elbows.
"Oso" means "bear" in the language we both
barely speak, but it is the only one we share.
It's what she calls herself. I don't know why.

She is the child-like lover of the jut-jawed Frenchman
(think of a centaur, priapic and coarse,
bathed in cologne and three times her age;
yet handsome, in a Rubirosa way)
who owns the penthouse in the building
where my wife and I rent month by month.

The two of us would study the two of them
in the elevator, and they would do the same,
and we fantasized about them, and we assumed
they did of us—two men, two striking Asian women,
in that tiny space—but we never spoke or nodded.
You don't start conversations in elevators.
New York rules. Paris rules. Big city stuff.

And then one day she seemed to be alone,
and, just a few days later, so was I.
The Frenchman was in Antwerp I gathered—

something to do with the diamond business.
He would be back in time for the World Cup.
And me? A brief assignment to turn around
a failing business had saved the company,
but destroyed what was left of a troubled marriage.
My wife was back in New York with her painting,
her friends, her lovers, her stylish *Japaneseness*.
I basked in the shards of a ruined relationship,
and learned a word or two of Vietnamese.

The Shawl

A faded woolen shawl—parched golds and reds—
sprawls across the couch. Precisely placed,
it hides all signs of age with style and ease
and just the slightest hint of decadence.
But lightly move the shawl, and burns and stains
and ends of threads emerge from where it was,
or turn it over and it's pocked with holes.

At night my wife and I will share the space
(she often wraps herself within the shawl)
to watch the newscasts and their endless bawl—
the threats, the fears, corruption, blame, disgrace,
the zealots and the damned, the dumb, the dead—
and when they're done we realign the shawl,
hide every stain and flaw—and so to bed.

To an Old Friend Who Died Young

The first time was a game, we all agreed,
a cry for help, of course, but nothing more,
and then you dove out over 87th Street.

The maid was due at noon—you gambled she'd
smell gas as soon as she came near the door—
that first time was a game. We all agreed

you missed your ex; you shrugged, you blamed the weed
and promised us there would be no encore—
but then you broke apart on 87th Street

that Sunday morning. What voices did you heed,
what madness crept up to the 14th floor?
The first time was a game, we all agreed;

we spoke of how you always seemed to need
attention; called up stunts you'd staged before—
and then you sailed out over 87th Street,

and gave the game an ending guaranteed
to make it clear who kept the final score.
The first time was a game, we all agreed;
and then you plummeted to 87th Street.

A Letter of Complaint to World War Two

In my life I have loved two women
and you knew them both before I did:
seduced one and tried to kill the other.

Sachiko adored you.
Her father a Tokyo mafioso, a gang boss, a *yakuza;*
you must have been proud of him, he
followed that Rising Sun
that big old blood red meatball
through Mongolia and Singapore, later
ran military construction in Taiwan.
Your air raids were wonderful.
Everybody fussed over her in the shelters.
She always had extra toys.
One of my father's aides
took me to the hospital every day,
to sing for the wounded soldiers.
I jumped from bed to bed
until they clapped and cheered.
I'm sure they hated me.
When you were over
the family was repatriated to Kyushu,
an area you had savaged.
No homes, barely any food.
One day a new girl came to school
in a bright yellow dress
carrying a shiny tin lunch box stuffed with
freshly made rice balls,
American candy.
Those other kids
beat the shit out of me
and the teacher helped.
Tore my dress apart. Smeared
mud and dirt all over me.

Took my lunch.
Called my father a criminal.
Now she is Spike.
Lives alone in Manhattan
paints large canvases
will not talk to other Japanese
but still speaks of you fondly.

Marta was born on the Baltic Sea,
in a house on a beach
behind a strip of pines
in front of a birch forest;
descended from the
Northern warrior women.
Do you remember?
You shot at her in 1939, asshole,
on the way to Saxony,
and again three years later
crossing a river below Munich,
helping her parents push a hand cart
through Europe.
Her father spoke six languages
ran a DP camp, forged the papers
that took them here.
Marta learned unaccented English within one year,
willfully disremembering Latvian and German.
We were born one week apart.
I remember you perfectly:
every victory, every scrap metal drive.
She will not recall your face
except when pictures of refugees and wagons
fleeing Saigon
Kosovo
Somalia

flash on a screen without warning.
But we are here and you are not.
We have outlived you,
my warrior woman and I,
my fierce pagan love.

The Sculptor, Dead at Age 34, and Her College Admirer

Beautiful and dark,
with a vague foreign accent,
she never looked at me.

I joined the literary group to meet her
and passed around my bullfight poem
which was all lower case
with the perfect last line
about mister death.

She said it was derivative,
and for three or four days
I thought that was a compliment.

Her rope sculptures hang
in the Whitney and the Tate.
An obituary said
she loathed being called
beautiful.

A Sestina for Bernie Madoff

To know just when to buy, and when to sell
is how I've been successful—knock on wood—
but looking wealth and fortune in the eye,
without admitting God's good work, won't work:
I serve my God, and though I'm not a *Talmid
Chacham*—no scholar, as we say—I've seen
enough of life, and every complex scene,
to know that those He chooses to excel
must always be more generous than timid.

New York, Miami, Boca, Hollywood—
it's all the same—I watch the folks who work
with me on charities, and that's how I
could tell at once that we'd see eye-to-eye—
it's turned out just the way I had foreseen.
My special Funds? They're private, and we work
with heavy players only—a tight-knit cell
that minds its business—but my friends would
all be pleased with you, and you'd fit in amid

the group. Suppose that we arrange a mid-
range first investment that would nicely lie
within your comfort level? The Street would
hear some buzz about a new face on the scene.
There's more we do, of course, than buy and sell—
a rabbi has at least two hats—so if we work
things out, perhaps in time your charm could work
for us. And if you have misgivings, God forbid,
you're always free to reach me on my cell.

The single most important thing that I
impress upon my clients is that I'm seen
to be a righteous man—not made of wood,
of course, but flesh and blood—who never would
betray my God, or those with whom I work.
So what you're saying now is quite obscene!
I've spent my life in helping others pyramid
their earnings, and it breaks my heart that I
must sadly say there's nothing left to sell.

Oh yes, I broke some rules so it would work—
I was the eye inside the Pyramid—
all seeing, yet unseen. Please call my cell.

Note:

The form is a sestina, disguised in keeping with the poem.

50

II.

A Portrait of Gorian Dreigh

A Portrait of Gorian Dreigh

His friends and colleagues envy Gorian Dreigh—
prolific poet with a rugged look
that's perfect for the flyleaf of a book—
he's thickened over time, his hair's now gray,
but the thing that makes it all so strange is
year after year, his photo never ages.

Biblical Insights Through the *New York Times* Crossword Puzzle

The Thursday clue was "Son of Genesis",
so automatically I entered Seth,
for Seth—poor unsung Seth—has always been
my favorite Bible guy: he languisheth
almost unknown, unclaimed; a silhouette
and little more among the Abels, Cains,
begetters and begat, whose lives and deaths
get all the ink. He never killed a brother;
no *East of Eden in the land of Nod*
promotion trips: Seth didn't know from rains
or reigns, he had no agent, took no pains.

So in went SETH. In ink, and boldly writ,
the way I do. The letter count was right—
that's all I checked—but I liked the way it fit
and sensed that Seth would finally get some light;
that Adam's unassuming third son might
be freed at last from his obscurity,
for Seth is nothing but a *mensch* to me.

But once the crosswords came to cross it came
across that SETH would never ever work.
I crossed him out, and wrote in CAIN the way
that I rewrite—in extra heavy ink—
and then the vision came—it's ABEL that
they want! The Times has always been my God,
and God has always moved to favor ABEL.
How sad, and utterly predictable:
the thoughtful, brown-nosed son gets picked again—
an Upper West Side choice—so very *Times*.
I enter ABEL—with a thick red pen—
and pray that Seth and I will meet again.

Tina

The smell is always there—the noisy guys
themselves of course, all sweat and strong cologne,
the greasy chicken wings, the beer, the hair
spray everywhere. *I swear to God,* says Tina,
the dumbest ones of all wear Harley tees—
ask any girl—just take a fucking poll—

the deejay signals, and she takes the pole;
dry humps it, blows some kisses to disguise
a little yawn, and then it's time to tease—
to get it going on her carnal own—
until the throbbing music ceases Tina
will caress herself and throw her hair

at jerks who think a strand of pubic hair,
a snatch of snatch, a thatch, a shining pole
is where God lives; and dream of Princess Tina—
Tina-Tina-hot-Latina, big, big, eyes,
brown sugar thighs—as theirs and theirs alone.
And Tina knows all their propensities.

She does her *fuck-me-fuck-me-fuck-me* tease,
goes upside down, and splits and spins, her hair
cascading down. The runway's hers alone,
as Tina slithers down the rabbit pole,
click-clacks her five-inch spikes right in some guy's
round face, and sighs. *The gig's half done,* frets Tina—

where's Lancelot, all hot to possess Tina?
She scopes the goons and loons and Mr. T's—
a sucker can be spied in any guise.
Fatty there in front with slicked-back hair?
Private couch dance for your private pole?
Help a college girl repay a loan?

55

A piece of meat who thinks he's Sly Stallone
pulls out a bankroll that surprises Tina:
Stay with me, Rocky, till I'm off the pole;
we'll get a Private Room, and no more tease.
The champagne's awesome, and I love your hair.
I know you aren't like the other guys.

And me? I wash my hair. Despise the guise
I twist around a pole. I live alone.
I work on my moralities, says Tina.

The Elders

The city bosses and their smoke-filled rooms
gave us Roosevelt, Truman, Eisenhower;
and once you get beyond cigars and booze,

the smell of Scotch and misbegotten power,
there's still the knowledge that those drunken fools
picked out Roosevelt, Truman, Eisenhower.

But now we've fixed the system, passed new rules—
the people choose their leaders, not some hacks,
(and all acknowledge that those party tools

were mostly focused on each other's backs).
Today, the public's voice is clear and loud—
the people choose their leaders, and the hacks

just keep the score, and we can all be proud
that this is when democracy can flower.
Indeed, the public's voice is clear and loud:

the rule of law has fundamental power.
But every night that inner tune resumes:
The city bosses and their smoke-filled rooms
gave us Roosevelt, Truman, Eisenhower.

The Candidate Makes a Public Statement
on a Private Matter, His Wife at His Side

There's something in the rules, I guess, to make
them brave the scene, dead pale, beside the jerk,
because they all endure it; none will shirk
the role, not one has said, *Give me a break,*
you asshole, can't you tell how much I ache—
you're on your own—instead, she takes her place
and stands there, shaking, life drained from her face
as hubby asks the world for time and space.

There is no way, José, I am forewarned,
you'd ever see me shame myself like that.
I change the channel, give her knee a pat,
suppress a little joke on women scorned.
I'd like to think she'd stand by me, but still,
I've never run for office, never will.

Is Good Life

WASHINGTON...*they had lived more than a decade in American cities and suburbs where they seemed to be ordinary couples...on Monday federal prosecutors accused 11 people of being part of an espionage ring...*NEW YORK TIMES

Is good suburban life in Montclair Falls—
the kids are fine—Natasha says hello—
but Moscow Center will not take my calls.

Each day I gather findings in the malls,
and send report, so Kremlin guys can know
of good suburban life in Montclair Falls:

A super autumn sale on alcohols!
New classes soon will start in Tae Kwan Do!!
But Moscow Center will not take my calls,

or golf club bills, or other wherewithals
to meet right people. It takes horn to blow
for good suburban life. In Montclair Falls

you must wear fancy clothes, not overalls,
and children's piano lessons are not low,
but Moscow Center will not answer calls.

I practice craft, stuff messages in walls,
work hard for paying such big bills we owe.
In good suburban life in Montclair Falls

you cannot have too many Hermes shawls—
all Natasha's friends have told her so—
but Moscow Center will not take my calls,

and both old Chevvies must have overhauls.
Natasha asks car salesman friend to show
us good Suburban. Life in Montclair Falls,

she bawls, is not for guy without big balls,
and says I must insist we need more dough.
But Moscow Center not returning calls.

And now I find Natasha has the galls
to pack five bags, and tell me she will go.
Was good suburban life in Montclair Falls,

but Omsk has shops, and healthy outdoor stalls,
and my Natasha loves the taste of snow.
Was good suburban life in Montclair Falls;
the FBI was pleased to take my calls.

Flag Day

It arrived in eighty star-flecked crates
in a caravan of sixteen trucks
with eagles painted on the doors
and an Honor Guard of Boy Scouts, Girl Scouts

and the Veterans of All Wars
marched with them from the depot
to the fields past Table Mountain
where the FLAG would be assembled and displayed;

held horizontal
not allowed to touch the ground

rippling very slightly as the expert holders agitated it:
the largest GIANT FLAG that ever was,
larger than a dozen football fields;
a cathedral, it was said, of fabric, rope, and blood and pride.

Those who spent their lives amidst great flags
and multitudes of flags,
who wore flag pins, tattoos and flag insignia,
who loved the flags that flew at sports events

and auto sales and jumbo stores; who spent their time at
rallies where the flags were stacked in staggered tiers
that swept across great rows of uniforms; and thrilled to portraits
of the flag-draped faces of their leaders and their leader's wives

who roared as drums accompanied
The Entrance of the Flags
even these, the oldest, flag-wise, flag-ennobled
townsfolk all agreed that this was special and unique

that their GIANT FLAG would dwarf all other flags
that ever waved or stretched or ever were
and that this day would not be soon forgotten.

        .   .   .

With practiced skill
as quick as flight
the site was organized
and interlocking light

blue tarps staked down to form a shield
for there was danger here:
if a calamity occurred,
if the GIANT FLAG should drop upon the ground
IT WOULD HAVE TO BE IMMEDIATELY DESTROYED—
but accidental, fleeting contact with a plastic sheet
would be acceptable.

        .   .   .   .

Eighty crates were spaced out on the tarps
and work began; starting from the center,
stretching, holding, joining sections
spreading out the nation's colors as the nation once had spread—
and almost from the start the strain began to show
upon the expert holders—

huge men, men who worked on farms and in the mills
biceps and shoulder muscles humped like bulls
heels dug in, leaning backwards
almost parallel to the ground

great forearms quivering to keep the GIANT FLAG
from touching even plastic: too proud to ask for help.
But help was needed, and as the FLAG dipped dangerously
the Volunteer Town Firemen, unasked, unspoken, rose as one

and squatted, skittered, duck-walked underneath the FLAG—
thick-bodied men who carried hose through burning buildings,
ducking low to breathe pure air, they were ideal for this task.
The FLAG continued growing, the holders spread more thinly now

and the Police Auxiliary slid under the rippling silk and canvas
as others grabbed the edges
the entire high school football team
and the Boy Scouts and Girl Scouts

doctors and lawyers, housewives, store clerks, ministers,
factory workers, farmhands,
a baker still smelling of cinnamon and yeast,
holding up the GIANT FLAG, keeping it unsullied, sacrosanct
and the word spread, and those beneath the flag all knew

and the few remaining on the sidelines understood
that underneath the flag the light that filtered through
and blended all the streams and shades and colors of the nation
was beautiful. And well worth any sacrifice.

At last, the FLAG was stretched,
the holders screaming in triumphant pain
the multitudes beneath its silk and cotton span
each sharing in the task
                    and then

with crowd and fabric tensed and trembling
the signal was emitted to initiate the
                    FLYOVER

Four silver jets came streaking over treetops, directly from the east
the sun behind them stark and white
a noise above, a roar and they were gone—
four contrails arcing gracefully like flowers in a vase

and visible for just a blink, a micro-second, when—
the ground erupted in a fire ball that swallowed
FLAG and fields, holders, volunteers, and spectators
that reached six thousand feet!

            .   .   .

Intensive inquiries were launched, of course
investigations, hearings, testimony to Committees:
a chemical reaction, possibly; a compound in the tarpaulin
or glue that added strength to silk, released by heat beneath the
FLAG

a static spark set off the gas
a bomb was buried in the grass
there was a man who saw a silver object falling from the final jet
the sunlight glinted as it tumbled, he was sure of that

and strangers camped near Table Mountain
in the weeks before the incident, were gone—
they had received a phone call, it was said, and disappeared
and whispers claimed no silver jets were sent to fly that day

no records of the pilots' names
no documents. no trace
no reasons for the signal lights
some noticed in the hills.

The hearings carried on,
executives were called to testify, and experts in their fields
and what was first decided was to raise a monument:
a Study Group took over, and their meetings soon began.

Above *Fat Papa's* Bar in Casablanca

Café on the veranda: Ilsa sleek,
her hair now set off by a silver streak,
as beautiful as ever, still a chic
and polished avatar of high-boned cheek.

The room appeared as if we'd spent a week
in bed instead of just one night—the reek
of sex and flat champagne, two flutes, all shriek
of carnal, sweat-drenched, sweet reunion; pique
my appetite for more.
                But she seems bleak:
"It won't work, Rick. You've lost the old mystique,
and turned into an aging film-crazed geek—
a droning and obsessive one-note freak."
The French doors close, but not before I speak,
We'll still have Paris, kid, and that was magnifique!

The Gallery Opening

"I really like the subtle use of negative,
um, space, you know, in contrast with the positive,
so that it all begins to seem so relative
and consequently, if I may, evocative—
which is precisely why it's so informative—
provocative, and at the same time tentative;
not in the least judgmental, not competitive,
but kind of, sort of like, almost illustrative.

"Collector? That sounds so accusative!
I'm just—you know—a bored executive
who sometimes buys some art. Conservative,
of course, and nothing too prohibitive.
And you? I see that you're not talkative.
I love that in a woman. Sensitive!"

Painted Women

1.

The first one was the Botticelli girl—
pre-Raphaelite, a Venus Lite whose ropes
of golden hair drew sparrows from the rooftops
when she glided down East Second Street;
and he—black leather cap, black coat, black beard,
small body twisted like a question mark—
appeared to stumble in her wake, appended
and dependent, yet somehow in charge.

And soon we saw her in the canvases
that lined his loft, and filled a gallery:
she rose up from a taxicab in one,
a Hudson River clamshell in another;
a hand half-hid her naked, perfect breasts.
The paintings were unframed: no glitz, no gilt;
just stretchers, staples, gesso and acrylic—
and her—the light brown eyes, that realm of hair.

His work sold quickly, then she disappeared
from studios, from Second Street, from life.
She left no baggage; no one knew her name.
Word got around from time to time that he
was spotted uptown somewhere, maybe Chelsea,
with a darker, yet familiar face.

2.

He reappeared, in time, beside a darker
yet familiar face, whose oval shape—
head cocked, brows plucked and arched above pursed lips—
was perched and angled on a neck so long
its very length became irrational.
We climbed four flights to reach his sublet loft
and poked around while she looked past our stares;
at ease and naked as she posed for him.

Modigliani Ronnie we anointed her,
we inbred elders of the neighborhood;
and watched, and shook our heads as, once again,
a stream of portraits of his newest love—
thin waist, broad hips, suggestive tufts of hair
beneath her outstretched and columnar arms;
or clothed and in a chair—engulfed our side-street
framing shops and filled the Avenues.

And when this batch was sold, then Ronnie too
had had her moment, had her flash of life,
and was not seen again. A thick Botero
girl with massive thighs moved in next year;
a Renoir, then a Balthus, then some more.
The gossip had it that his beard turned gray.

3.

His beard turned gray, then white, the story went.
Now he found his models on the street
and focused on an inch or two of skin.
He wore thick glasses as he stabbed on paint
throughout the progress of an afternoon,
and moved in closer, squinting through a lens;
the model, dozing, sprawled across a chair,
reduced to pixilated dots and dabs
as he enlarged each pore, each untweezed hair
that curled and wandered near an areole,
until the canvas spread to fill the room.

Until he was consumed in its enormity,
until *their* presence drained the room of air,
the folds and crush of belly, breast and flank
embracing, crushing and devouring him.
Or so the theory went when he had vanished,
when nothing could be found within the loft
except the paintings, stretched from wall to wall
and to the ceiling, of flesh and flesh and flesh,
so magnified and moist it seemed to breathe;
and stacks of massive rolls of canvases
that, unrolled, hinted of his tortured frame.

4

He had evaporated, evanesced,
the tortured frame a memory at best.
The painter and his many works and models
melted from the art scene and the Village.
But, yes, the waitress in this coffee shop
does have a Gaugin kind of look and style,
and the couple that just walked in holding hands,
and trade small kisses as they take a table,
bring Ronnie and the Botticelli girl
to mind. And is it just the low-cut dress
that makes that blonde barrista Rubenesque?

You see them drifting through the narrow streets
and in the markets and the laundromats,
these curiously familiar, striking women.
Some claim that if you try an angled glance
you may, at times, catch just the flicker
of a leather cap, a coat, a beard,
a body twisted like a question mark.

Waiting

I loved a dancer once, who had a great
audition look in lime green baggy tops
above rehearsal tights and hacked-off socks—
but when she found she couldn't elevate,
she shucked the toe shoes and their painful box,
and me as well—a shrug, a change of heart.
Now modern dance adores her barefoot grace,
and she and her new outdoor sculptor mate
preside together at his openings,
among the steel plates and thrusting beams.
I'm there as well—I'm often at their place—
and sense she hates the way he dominates
each group he's in, and brags about his art
and how he's in the Modern and the Tate.

She left me for a welder with a scar
above one eye; a man with hands like axe-
heads, and a SoHo loft with planked and black-
stained floors almost the size of Central Park.
I phone her frequently: we're still good friends
and talk of books and such, and I attend
their parties, full of girls and caviar.
I'll meet with him, in fact, this coming week—
she set it up—so he can see my script.
What I now need are contacts, not critique,
a lead to someone to produce the play,
some help to make up for the time that's slipped.
Meanwhile, I'll keep the day job, as they say;
it's not so bad, between the tips and pay.

At the Waldorf

Waldorf Astoria Hotels & Resorts today unveils its new global advertising campaign, "The Stories Begin Here," featuring international actress Olga Kurylenko. In the campaign, Kurylenko plays a character named Alexandra, created exclusively for her, as a young, successful and well-traveled couturier, spending time experiencing unforgettable moments at a Waldorf Astoria hotel. (From a press release.)

Taut in five inch heels and a jersey shift,
she stalks and sweeps across the lobby floor.
The fabric magnifies the thrust of hip,
and thigh, and turns her walk into the stroll
an elegantly tailored matador
would slowly take until the crowd was hushed—
and then confront the bull to smell its fear.
She loves to play these games of hotel lust:
the feints, the steady stare, the teasing dance, the thrust.

He appears to gaze back cautiously,
uneasy with the boldness in her glance,
unsure of where to look, or just what she
might have in mind, or why her studied stance
seems somehow more than interest or romance.
He fumbles with his tote-bag and his phone:
A hooker? At the Waldorf? Not a chance!
But what's her game? She's gorgeous, and alone:
it's just that stare that makes the prospects so unknown.

He nods, and breathes the briefest of hellos—
and all at once the lobby seems to teem
with women of a matching look and pose.
Where there was one, there's now a constant stream
of bold, alluring beauties; and their gleam
pervades the Waldorf, carnal yet refined.
It seems the hotel has a new regime.
The future rattles in the corners of his mind—
now men will have to walk a step behind.

I feel for this poor young man. No one warned him
of the Waldorf's bright new PR pitch
and the fearless and successful women
I've invented, or the hints of glitz
and worldliness that are my special niche.
It's all my fault, I guess. I'm good with flash
(my novel, on the other hand's, a bitch).
I write more nonsense, pour another splash.
If truth be told, I absolutely need the cash.

Toy Soldiers

The little tin men in their little tin hats
bang their loud little drums for the blood they won't shed;
and the ones who don't fight lead the rat-a-tat-tats
when the little tin men in their little tin hats
fill the air with their calls like a clatter of cats—
until nothing is left but the rats and the dead,
and the little tin men with their little tin hats,
and their loud little drums, and the blood that's been shed.

Wabberjocky

The in and out transformed to on and off,
her wabberjocky jockey went to sea
with shockleshells and writhyrambs, while she
frick-frocked with scrumptious scullions in the froth;
and wondered if she should become a polymorph.
Returned, he donned his swanned *Manteau de Nuit,*
found sleeves cuffed back, hem shortened tidily,
and grobbled with his breakfast back and forth.

You've slogged another woman, or a dwarf:
the scrumpsome dwarf, the dwarfsome dwarf who hides
beneath the bridge he said, and blissed her thighs
until the urchlings screamed for honey broth.
They cried and skied and neither realized
that each loved each as candles love the moth.

1001 Ovillejos

"There are, my Lord," the slave girl said,
      in bed,
"One thousand poems I can recall.
      They're all
on varied forms of sex: I claim
      the same
great skills in love as verse; and came
with joy tonight—and will each night."
She smiled, and thought, with fists clenched white,
      In bed, they're all the same.

In bed they're all the same, but still
      I will
keep freedom as my final goal,
      control
whatever forces might debate
      my fate.
I know just how to hide my hate
and focus on the here, the now;
be governed by my slave girl vow:
      I will control my fate.

I will control my fate. I'll school
      this fool.
This arrogant and loud-mouthed fake
      will make
me great, he says. And then he'll ditch
      me. Rich
with tapes and drama, I won't bitch.
You'll hear him beg for discipline,
whimper within his orange skin.
      This fool will make me rich.

Reflections on a Fib

If
you
begin
with a fib
there is no choice but
to chase the hump-backed, spiral path
that wayward words have led you into since creation.

I've heard of ways to stumble back, one hand on a wall,
unbuild, unwind, undo, retract—
my way is to shrug—
make a joke
and let
things
lie.

Trochees Are the Perfect Fix

I love a line of trochees now and then.—David Berman

I love a line of trochees now and then.
Snort them up—my ear will tell me when
I'm due again—set for that metric hit—
the off-beat rush I need to discomfit
and chop the chain of pure iambic verse
that spreads a sonorous Shakespearean curse
across my winter sonnet's boring drone.

Trochees are the poet's perfect fix—stone
fences that provide a periodic high
to lift a rhyme through dull New England sky
to a caesura; punctuate the hills
with jig-saw boulders, frozen silver spills
of rock, the drift of snow on wind-tossed
lake, two paths uncrossed, a touch of frost.

Memoirs of a Finalist

These days, I'm frequently a finalist—
short-listed, as the British like to say—
a nominee, a candidate, a *mensch!*
My bio glows with finalist acclaim.
I'm *a contender,* not a could-have-been,
well past the years of *woulda-shoulda-Brando-
Steiger* self-indulgent back seat whines.
That's why I am so often named a finalist.

We are a special group, we finalists;
our bodies gleam, we shake out arms and legs
to loosen muscles, pace within our lanes.
We chatter back and forth with knowing winks,
strike poses, and ignore the banks of cameras.
We're trim, we're thin, our hair cascades in ringlets;
the men have leather patches on their elbows,
and drop designer's names without a wink.
The women's breasts are bared, or barely there;
each one of us is poised to glide or saunter
down the aisle, and don a sash and wreath.
But somehow I have never made that trip,
not loped the winner's lope, have never thanked
my producer, trainer, wife, director,
and all those scores of little dickhead people.
Am I *too frequently* a finalist,
a wasted prince who cannot wear the crown,
perhaps the victim of an ancient curse
from a forgotten, buried incident?

Years and years and slapped-past years ago
on routine travel in another life,
a handsome and familiar stranger
boarded a Darien commuter train
and shared my brace of ersatz leather seats.
The iridescent TV star who sang
to Miss America each year, who ran
the Beauty Pageant from Atlantic City,
who sent the winner on her runway stroll,
who hugged and comforted the runners-up,
presided over tears and shattered hopes
(and, though it never struck me at that time,
a world authority on finalists)
was once my New York-bound companion.

The star did not remove his perfect jacket,
nor his perfect smile. His legs remained
uncrossed, his collar closed. He sat erect,
arms at his sides. His undefiled skin
was of an orange shade not found in nature.
His teeth gave off a glow like radium.
The rich, black hair swept back, and then was cropped
precisely at his collar, nesting there,
dense and impregnable, contained in place
by potions never sold to common souls.
I was flattered. This august man had walked
the aisle, checking every seat and face,
and had selected me as someone who
he knew would know the codes of privacy,
would never try to start a conversation
or, even worse, request an autograph.

We sat in manly silence, side by side,
and all went well until Grand Central Station.
Folding up the Times, *I clumsily spilled*
the remnants of my coffee on his perfect
trouser leg. Disaster! *Magically,*
a pure white hankie sprouted in his hand,
he dabbed it at the blue-black lustrous fabric
and darkness swallowed dark, no stain remained.
I made the proper noises—he said nothing—
but at last he looked directly at me.
I stared right back—a contact was established,
and something moved behind the orange mask:
a brief communication had been issued
and what the message seemed to say was "earthworm".

Always a bridesmaid, never a bride,
as some fool said. And where did it go wrong?
I am so frequently a finalist,
but never had that one quick smell of fame.
Is it the spleen of all those shattered ranks
who had to paste on smiles and watch the winner
walk her joyous and triumphant walk
that passed to me when he and I locked eyes,
and festers still? Did the plastic bastard
screw me up for all eternity?
Perhaps it's just bad luck, the odds and such.
At any rate, I've put it out of mind,
and all I ask is that you cast your vote,
for me, for Miss Congeniality.

Refractions

A sentence is a sound in itself on which other sounds called
words may be strung. —Robert Frost

A sentence is a sound upon which other sounds are strung—
                a temple bell, an ancient gong,
    a voice that owns the wind and night and cuts into the bones,
      the agonies and memories of songs that once were sung—
a sentence is a golden string
                        upon which sounds are hung.

So much depends upon *upon*; upon the way it drones.

A sentence is a monochrome against which words are flung—
                an unrolled scroll, a whitewashed stone,
        a canvas primed for undertones
        of what was known and what was seen,
                        the sense an angled view can
                        bring
to clarify the stammering
                    a voice emerges from.

A sentence is a crowd of sounds that can be made to sing.

III.

The *Tummler*

Rush Hour

The guy is taking up at least five seats
on the crowded el train to the Bronx.
Rush hour. Sweating bodies jammed together,
briefcases, shopping bags, no room to read,
but there's a bit of space around the man.
Nobody gets too close. You never know.
"He's drunk" a standing woman says, and sighs.
All I can see are polished shoes reposing
on the bench, and a dark blue business suit.

I was almost thirteen, and returning
home from Yankee Stadium on *Succos,*
which was my favorite Jewish holiday—
so big you didn't have to go to school,
but not enough to go to synagogue.
I'd promised my mother I'd be home by four,
And then I waited by the players' exit
for autographs—and lost all track of time.
I'll tell my mother it was extra innings,
but I knew she'd bring this up for weeks:
"Where *were* you? A boy is *two hours* late?"

By Tremont Avenue the crowd had thinned,
and no one had to stand next to the drunk
who rolled over, still snoring and asleep.
His fedora was now pillowing his head,
a Countess Mara tie was pinned in place,
and I recognized the pin-striped suit
he alternated with the solid blue.
No need to see his face. It was my father.

What surprised me was that I was not
surprised. I always knew he always drank.
My parents fought about it every night.
It was on his breath when he came home,
late for dinner almost every evening—
under all the cigarettes and Sen-Sen,
and chewing gum—and then he started pouring
Chivas as soon as she had gone to bed.
I was the boy who was not there.
When my parents had a screaming match
in the kitchen at two in the morning—
about money, this time, as well as drinking—
I lay in my room on the other side of the door
and lost myself in *The Naked and the Dead*.
Life was school, stickball, basketball,
and four books a week from the public library.

But now this thing had happened where I had
to make a choice. I quickly understood.
My father drunk and sleeping through his stop
almost every night, riding to the end of the line
at Woodlawn Cemetery, being roused
by the train crew and shuffled over
to the other side to get the train back down.
That would add at least an hour to the trip.
And maybe sometimes he'd drop off again,
and wake again in Coney Island.

Only two more stops to Kingsbridge Road.
What to do? Do I wake him up or not?
If we show up together, would my mother
forget about my coming home that late?

And if I do wake him, what do I say?
What would he say? We almost never talked.
Do I simply pretend this never happened,
go home and wait for him to show up later,
continue living in my separate world?
I tapped his shoulder. And then again. Again.

The Holidays

They were there for me every fall,
hidden in September and October,
Crackerjack box prizes.
No school.
Days off.
Stickball in the schoolyard,
except for Yom Kippur. On Yom Kippur,
everybody stood in front of the synagogue.
My father wore his best suit,
strolled from group to group,
borrowed a ticket
to go inside and say the prayer for the dead.

After college I found a job and a car:
'53 Pontiac convertible, light green, cracked leather seats.
The next Yom Kippur I stayed home again.
Crisp Indian Summer day.
Starting early, I waxed and buffed that beautiful automobile
parked down the block, near the rabbi's house,
whispered to it and made it iridescent.
The elders of the neighborhood
flanking Rabbi Miller:
Allen Goldenberg's father
Irving Reiser's father
Michael Melnick's father
Dr. Shulman
emerged and descended the stairs.
"When the father died," I heard the rabbi say,
"They had the nerve to ask me
to speak at the grave."
I pounded Turtle Wax into the Pontiac,
moved to my own apartment the next month.

The *Tummler*

A second cousin I have never met,
determined to determine where we're from
has found me, somehow, through the internet;
and so my father's sister's daughter's son
and I have intermittently begun
checking *shtetl* lists for hints and clues
of who lived where in nineteen hundred one
in what was Poland, Russia, Belarus,
and gossiping of relatives and roots.

We come from Chomsk, we think, southwest of Minsk
and north of Pinsk: a dot upon a map
that shuddered each time borders were redrawn,
the locale for an old Borscht Belt routine—
"A man from Minsk meets a man from Pinsk
and a rabbi, on a train", the comic starts,
and the aging crowd begins to giggle,
certain they will hear a joke they know.
But the punch line is there is no line
for the comedian, the *tummler*, to spout—
no wink, no leer, no photographs of bearded
elders and their wives, no names. It ends
with a man from Minsk, and a man from Pinsk,
and a latitude and longitude,
and all we know is that one hundred years
ago one thousand Jews called Chomsk their home.
The Tsars kept perfect records, in their way.

> *"The Yiddish actor, Boris Timoshenko,*
> *is walking back from lunch at Rappaport's*
> *on Second Avenue in his mink-lined overcoat,"*
> the *tummler* resumes, *"and he sees this woman,*
> *and she sees him, and they smile at each other,*
> *and he's the famous Boris Timoshenko,*

so she goes with him to his hotel,
and they screw like hungry dogs all afternoon.
When she leaves she gets a goodbye kiss,
and a ticket to his show that night."

A family elder on my mother's side,
obliterates one half of the Ukraine
with his misshapen thumb: "Right there," he says,
"Shmul and Libby, Celia, Jake and Rose.
But Julius was from somewhere further south—
they called him The Turk because he was so dark."

When Grandpa Julius married Grandma Rose
they lived on Grand by Orchard: crowded space,
three rooms, a sink and stove, fourth floor, and those
three white-washed rooms became the only place
they spoke about when asked where we were from.
Before The Bronx we lived on Rivington,
Grandma would say, *and before that Grand.*
And stop. Before Grand there were only Cossacks.

"'What do I do with this?' the woman asks,
"I have hungry children crying at home.
A ticket? I need bread for my babies."
"'Bread?" he says "'You want bread, you fuck a baker!'"

Trapped in a golden ring on my left hand,
the last Tsar, face down, kisses my finger.
Ten rubles—an old double eagle coin—

minted in St. Petersburg in 1904,
the year of my father's birth in Chomsk,
before the hordes of Cossacks chased him here,
before the days of jokes and and *tummlers*.
Chased them all here. Horsemen wheel and dart.
Grand by Orchard was where life began.

Poem *Noir*

The trendy shades obscure the fact that she
is sixty. Her second husband, eighty-two,
is dying, inch-by-inch, beside the blue-
green tile Miami condo pool that he
is carried down to every day by two
Jamaican nurses, who agree that he,
betrayed by piss and prostate, wishes she
would simply let him be. Her *Gauloise* blue
silk scarf, the blonde and silver chignon she
affects, accent the tableau of the two
evading winter, hoping winter kills.
Fixed in the pose she sees to it that he
has shade, sighs to a friend in lighter blue,
"When my time comes, I have these little pills."

From the Memoirs of Mickey, the Busboy

I never was a full time Catskill rat—
those guys who work the mountains from mid-May
until a week or two past Labor Day;
help open up a place, rejoin old friends,
and slip two fifties to the maître de
to get a favored station by the windows
with every table looking at the lake—
reserved for regulars and solid tippers—
then take off for Miami, or Key West
and work the winter in some classy dive,
bopping waitresses, and sometimes guests.

For me it was a desperate summer job—
waiting tables, bussing, kissing ass,
and after dinner helping mop the floors;
then working at the hotel bar each night—
eighteen-hour days, seven days a week.
Did you see *Dirty Dancing?* Wasn't me.
I never had the time, and couldn't dance,
and rarely ever made it to the pool.
Some days I never even saw the sun.
So what? I buckled down and earned the cash
to get me through my final year at school—
and used my college smarts to learn a trade
they never taught in Physics 101.
The hotel bar was where the game was played.

Steve and I, and Sy from NYU—
good *boychiks,* if not quite Yeshiva boys
(Steve wore a yarmelkeh to boost his tips)—

95

would serve and pour and clear, as bar boys do,
and banter with the drunks, and laugh and smile,
and carry it all off with perfect style;
and no one saw our private winks and nods,
or realized how hard we really worked
to screw the hotel and its hordes of guests.
The trick is in the timing, as they say,
and timing's what we worked on every night.

So listen up while Mickey tells you how—
and if your answer is *it won't work now,*
because we have computers now, not pads
and little pencils, Mickey knows all that.
The secret's in the timing, not the time.

Here's how it worked—we took the guest's drink orders
and placed them all with Shmul, who ran the bar—
then we paid Shmul, and collected from the tables.
The difference between what we gave Shmul,
and what we got back from the guests was ours,
and supposedly that was what we earned.
A simple system, difficult to fail.
But Shmul (the owner's sweating son-in-law)
was not the sharpest pencil in the box.
We always placed our orders all together
(the trick is in the timing, like I said)
"Three Dewars, Shmul, a Pepsi and a Cuba"
"Martini, very dry, two Bloody Marys,
Chivas with a splash, a ginger ale."
"Four Chivas up—they want them right away"
Can you keep up with that, and make the drinks,
remember all the prices, do the math?

96

Shmul didn't have a chance. So we three helped
by calculating what we paid to him.
After all, we were all college boys,
and if twenty dollars' worth of drinks
got sold to us for thirteen-twenty-five,
well there's a lesson there, somewhere, for Shmul.
And then you turn around, and serve the guests,
and twenty bucks can sky to thirty-plus
That part is basic—nothing new to add.
You pad the bills you can—avoid the singles,
the older couples staring into space,
and groups of women, even if they're drunk.
Best of all are large and flowing crowds
where someone asked that you just "run a tab".
and there's an Irv or Morris drowning out
the other guys, and asking for the bill.

Rest assured—Irv or Morris cannot know
how much they've drunk, or who had what, or when.
Decide how much you think that it will take
before Irv has a stroke—add ten percent—
and give the man the bill. It always works.

The following summer I got my blah-blah-blah
degree and found a solid, real job,
a glowing future, and a huge pay cut.
We summer buddies stayed in touch a while.
Sy became a lawyer—no surprise.
But Steve invested in an eight-seat cab,
and started driving loads of passengers
up to the Catskills—seven bucks a pop—

and then he bought another, then four more,
but somewhere there I guess he sold them all,
because in time he ended up on Wall Street,
a hedge fund billionaire—or so I read.
We're out of touch for almost sixty years,
but I'm glad that someone's used the tricks we learned.
The secret's in the timing, not the time.

Waiting Room

Ninety-nine-years-and-nine-months old,
my mother and the hip she broke,
the hairline fracture from three weeks ago,
are in the doctor's waiting room,
reading *Vogue* together—
the Lady Gaga issue.
When she goes home she will finish
some leftover steak from The Palm.
She has buried two husbands—
the poor one and the rich one—
outlasted eight doctors,
two World Wars,
seventeen Presidents,
and is doing better than
The Ladies Home Journal,
McCall's, Redbook, Look and *Life.*

At my father's unexpected early funeral
(ice on the bridge, a weak guard rail)
his older sister Lena, raised in Minsk,
arrived with rented mourners.
The sound of their grieving,
bounced off trees and gravestones,
filling the cemetery,
as his mother threw herself
into the open grave,
and clung to the descending coffin,
screaming his name in Yiddish.
They dragged her out by the feet, displaying
layers of yards of black skirts,
mottled thighs.
My mother and I looked away.

At her second husband's funeral
a limousine scooped us up:
my wife and I in black and gray,
somber, but stylish;
an old friend of my mothers,
petite and blonde inside a navy coat;
and then my mother,
waiting in front of the Plaza
in tailored beige.

"This reminds me of an old joke,"
she said, and on the way to this funeral
she told the one about the rabbi
at a funeral in Williamsburg, beseeching
Who will say a good word for this man?
repeatedly into silence.
He was a member here for forty years.
Who will say a good word for Hyman Katz?
Finally, from the oldest congregant
a feeble response:
His brother was worse.

Both husbands were named Henry.
She claimed she only married Henrys
because she wasn't very good with names.
At Henry the Second's small graveside service
nobody had remembered
to arrange for a rabbi,
so we mourners shrugged,
and struggled through the *Kaddish* ourselves.
Most of us knew most of the words,

and we threw in a *Sh'ma* as well,
reflexively. You can't go wrong with the *Sh'ma.*
Sh'ma Yisrael, Adonai eloheinu, Adonai echad.
Hear O Israel, the Lord our God, the Lord is One.

"We should talk about Henry," a cousin said.
"He sure loved to eat," my mother responded,
"the man enjoyed his food."
And so we discussed Danny's Hideaway,
and how Henry devoured their lamb chops,
and the Grotta Azzurra on Broome Street
(which Henry called the Blue Grotto),
and The Rascal House and Wolfie's in Miami,
and how Henry would tip the corned beef guy
at Katz's on Delancey
to carve the sandwich only from the lean end.

After, we went to another cousin's apartment
off Broadway in the West Nineties,
and honored Henry with the very best,
with cheeses and bagels from Zabar's
and platters of whitefish, lox and sable
from Barney Greengrass The Sturgeon King.
"He never snored," the widow reminisced,
"and just had instant coffee in the morning."

With food and sideshows like this,
it pays to hang around.
My mother wants the walker handles set higher,
so she won't bend over like an old woman.
She'll tell the doctor when we see him.

A Memorial Service for My Mother, Age 102

A cousin may have had some work—the chin
looks tighter than before—her husband winces
when he stands, and Edie could not make
the drive, and this one's hair looks better gray,
and Sam is bent and Becca simply old.
All spy the shakes, the sags, the extra pounds—
the kind of hard-eyed observations *she*
would have made and noted gleefully.

So as we family gather for a Sunday
afternoon of memories and praise,
and hover over crackers, goat cheese, trout,
my generation checks each other out.
I fear the next convergence, when the plot
recasts to who is there and who is not.

The Rabbi's Wife

I am the *rebitzin,* the rabbi's wife.

I love the smell of Friday afternoons:
the food and freshly polished furniture,
rich soup I cooked the day before, and cooled—
beef and chicken, onions, fennel, herbs—
now strained, reheated, concentrated, seasoned;
the warmth of fresh-baked bread,
salt-crusted chicken fat, Israeli olives, oil—and me—
freshly cleaned and washed, damp from the bath.
I have anointed my body with lotions,
rubbed them luxuriously into thighs, legs, breast,
shaved and tweezed, perfumed myself,
put on a good silk blouse. The Shabbos earrings,
gleam like the silver on the table.
The skirt hangs nicely on my hips,
and now the face, the look, the tilt of head.
I am the *rebitzin,* the rabbi's wife.
He will be proud.

Did I tell you that at Brandeis I was voted
Least likely to become a rebitzen?
I always like to mention that;
it works to break the ice, to start a conversation,
and usually I'm the one to do it, though the fault is his—
he is too beautiful, my blue-eyed, tall Yeshiva boy,
that *shagitz* face, and with that name—
whoever heard of a Rabbi Jefferson? The school kids joke
we want our money back, the rebbe is a goy—
but it gets things going, and he knows enough to tell
of how his great-great-uncle took the name,
at Ellis Island. I drop in Harvard, and my PhD.

and talk about the teaching and my children's group,
how pleased I was the day he chose
the seminary over Princeton,
and cross my legs, and nod:
I am the *rebitzin,* the rabbi's wife;
what else is there to say?

Can I say his chest is hairless, but the mat
below his navel is luxuriant;
that I could see he was excited
the first time we started chatting in the Library;
that I had been watching him for weeks,
that his ear will bleed when I bite it,
that he had the tightest ass I'd ever seen,
that I don't care who said what at the Men's Club meeting,
that the other condo owners roll their eyes when he gets started,
that it takes him fifteen minutes to decide on breakfast,
that I know my thighs show when I cross my legs,
that I notice who noticed.
That there is a young man in my Wednesday yoga class
who moves like a cat, and has blonde curls down to his neck,
that I pinch the Shabbos candles out, and feel the pain,
and smell the dark and final curl of smoke?

I am the rebitzin, the rabbi's wife.

IV.

At Plover Island

Haibun: Plover Island

Plover Island is a fragile barrier beach that hovers in the Atlantic, north of Boston. A community of wind-and-sea-salt-blasted wooden houses hides in its sand and shrub brush. From October through April the water turns steel gray, and seals can be seen playing in the channel and sometimes on the beach. The summer people are gone. Those who choose to winter in a place like this do so willfully. They have been captured by the way the sea grass waves in the wind and then nestles under snow. They are infatuated with the damp brine and seaweed smell of mornings. They stand at dusk behind thick glass deck doors, and watch the low, dark storm clouds scud down from the north. They seek silence and solitude.

> *the surf, the moon*
> *and summer renters,*
> *drunk and loud*

The day after a heavy January storm buries the island it is totally silent. You cannot hear the wind. You cannot hear the surf. The house feels compressed by the immense weight of snow it bears. It is smaller, tighter. The flames of the wood stove push back the walls, keep us alive. We whisper. Outside, the noon landscape is whiteness, punctuated by a few small pines. I read Kawabata's *Snow Country* again. Beyond the bleached and frozen beach, the winter ocean waits, dead black.

> *gray-rimmed and bare,*
> *this pale midwinter beach*
> *lets gull bones bleach*

Summer Employment

The paper lady's long-limbed, red-haired daughter
speeds past us on her bike once school is out,
and weaves through beachfront streets like flowing water:

her summer job is Mom's delivery route—
so something bright that hints of something wild
streams past us on her bike when school is out—

the paper lady's shining, auburn child
bombards us with the *Times* and *Globe* and *News.*
as something bright calls out with something wild,

and golden skin and wind-swept cries infuse
the ocean air with untamed energy
not found within the *Times,* the *Globe,* the *News.*

The route complete, she plunges through the sea,
her body slick, wet seaweed in her hair;
the ocean charged with untamed energy.

We know that just as soon as she can dare,
the paper lady's long-limbed, red-haired daughter,
her body taut, wet seaweed in her hair,
will leave this island beach for deeper water.

At the Salt Marsh

Is it the Snowy Egret or the Great
that navigates the marsh this afternoon,
propelled by an antique Egyptian gait?

A refugee from Cleopatra's tomb,
arresting, solitary, slightly strange,
that moves across the marsh this afternoon

with all the elegance it can arrange.
Insanely white, with lacy snow-white plumes—
arresting, solitary, slightly strange,

it morphs to what my roving mind presumes—
an alabaster bird, a temple toy,
Insanely white, with lacy snow-white plumes—

and seems to take a slow and total joy
in putting on this undulating show:
this alabaster bird, this temple toy,

that makes it all beside the point to know
if it's the Snowy Egret or the Great,
(propelled by an antique Egyptian gait),
that's putting on its undulating show.

Tree Swallows in August

At first it all seems random, then each day
another group appears, till by degrees
their black-and-whiteness fills the Refuge skies
and scattered banks and swoops of anarchy
give way to groups that practice in-line, tree-
top passes—now swallows swarm and sweep in free
yet structured flight, now soar in symmetry:
two Escher flocks merge upward joyfully.

"Bank left," I shout, and tilt to show them how,
"Pull yourselves together—nose to tail—
THERE IS NO 'I' IN 'SWARM.'"
                                    Their Vee takes sail,
and on the Refuge road, I take a bow
to plaudits from the passing cars, then hear,
"That imbecile is back again this year."

Winter, 2013

Dead gray and February bleak;
no color on this frozen beach
relieves the ice-flecked sands that streak—
dead gray and February bleak—
to meet a black horizon, seek
the end of day where gull bones bleach
dead gray and February bleak.
No color lifts this battered beach.

On Rolfes Lane

Two bikers, slim, androgynous as ninjas
in matching, one-piece coal-dark racing leathers,
traded gestures, straddling twin vehicles.
Their low and lupine motorbikes displayed
twin snouts as I jogged past at six this morning;
two slabs of black, one slashed with brilliant green,
both peering from the private access road
which snakes out from a mass of juniper
between two fading white Colonials.

The graveled way where they were idling
curled and vanished as it sloped uphill,
the pines and lilacs that outlined it fading
into shadows and a hint of square-cut
hedge: I liked to think of it as leading
to a house that hid behind the others
on the Lane, and fantasized about
just who it was who chose the juniper,
or the poppies that arrived each Spring;
imagined academic types, perhaps,
retired, snuggled in with history books;
a kitchen rich with dried and powdered spice.

They rolled out to Rolfes Lane, accelerated
instantly, bodies quickly parallel
to their machines, each bike and rider fused
into a single, sculpted element.
Mute and faceless under tinted visors
the pair turned left in tandem at the light
and disappeared on High Street; here then gone.

What had been left behind them up that road
at six AM. Perhaps a thank you note?
A Bauhaus home? Or scrawls of blood on blood.
I run most mornings, scan the local paper—
New weekend parking rules. The Elks will meet.
Three piping plover chicks seen on the beach—
and pray tomorrow's is as dull as ever.

Bookshop

Her mass of graying hair, loose shirt and jeans,
fit well among the rows of books and shelves.
The man seems odd, however—ill at ease
and frowning as he moves a step too close.
She hears his breathing, sees him close his eyes.
I know that scent, he whispers, *Opium?*
That's it, she quickly says, and slides away,
rejoins her husband, and relates, bemused:
I think some guy may just have hit on me.

In Poetry? Between the C's and G's?
She sketches out the little interchange,
and he responds with riffs and fantasies.

The man had recognized his dead wife's fragrance.
But better yet—a master parfumeur,
beguiling women with his ancient skills,
seeking out the solitary ones.
he inhaled all their truths and essences:
"It seems you have been doing certain things."
Or possibly a simple specialist,
he only knew Dior and St. Laurent,
and sought out women of a certain age.

She has no urge or time to play those games,
but thinks it's not so bad, at sixty-plus,
when someone takes the time to make a pass.

At Plover Island, 9/28/01

Dust, smoke, hats, flags, voices, noise
The set is on all day, there are no commercials

I soak the last garlic greens from my wife's garden
in water from the sea,
set them steaming on a hot grill,
layer on thin half moons of bright lemon,
fresh black trout, quickly cleaned and gutted,
their mouths and eyes open,
tuck ears of buttered corn between the fish
and cast handfuls of coarse sea salt over it all.

As I close the lid on the Weber
I think of the Shinto priest almost forty years ago
blessing the new factory at Totsuka,
droning, in a stiff white kimono,
scattering handfuls of salt to the wind,
purifying;
and of sumo wrestlers,
giant Kashiwado with the pimpled ass,
my favorite,
throwing salt as they glowered at each other.

It will all be finished in ten minutes,
the greens dry and charred, ashes;
the trout cooked through, moist and tender,
some of the corn kernels scorched and caramelized.
I will make a quick ponzu sauce—
shoyu and lemon juice and rice vinegar.
A salad is ready, slivered fennel and shitaké
smelling of earth,
focaccia for the Friday evening blessing.

And my wife and I will light candles, say prayers,
pluck all the trout flesh from the bones,
she delicately, using knife and fork
in the European style; I with my fingers,
drink much too much white wine,
and go to bed very early.
She will try to dream of her daughter, in the hills past Santa Fe,
and I of priests and sumo wrestlers.

They have begun to pull down the steel
filigree of death
soon there will be only a hole.

Lament

A day or two ago I tried to quote
Camus on modern man: *He defecates*
and reads the Sunday papers I first wrote—
but what it should have been was "fornicates",
and "Sunday" was my fantasy. So this
is what it all comes down to—thoughts of shits
and weekends with the *Times* invade a kiss-
kiss-fuck-fuck-bang-bang mind as age submits
his calling card, engraved, upon a bone-
white plate: a view ahead of weekly crossword
strugglings, and bits and scenes from well known
films, and scraps of other voices, overheard
as life retold: *He grows old*. I grow old,
and treasure all these things, and fear the cold.

The Historian

He always liked to battle with the dead—
philosophers and thinkers, poets, kings—
and pick apart the lives they said they led.
He found that if you battle with the dead—
(and the longer dead the better, as he said),
it allowed one to control the flow of things.
He always won his battles with the dead:
philosophers and thinkers, poets, kings.

His trick was to assume that nothing's true—
just question all—perfect a stance that flings
philosophers and thinkers, poets, kings,
out like a stack of chewed up chicken wings.
His reputation came from slashing through
philosophers and thinkers, poets, kings.
The game was to pretend that nothing's true.

But after many years he reached a place
where past had swallowed present; and he knew
his game of simply stating nothing's true
had won him tenure and a prize or two,
but in the end the pose had lost all grace.
He'd started by pretending nothing's true,
and after many years had reached that place

where lives will go when little truth is said.
His colleagues found him wearing, gave him space
(despite the years in which he'd earned his place).
An absent wife, ungrateful kids, a trace
of stumbles when he left the morning bed.
For after many years he'd found that place
where lives will go when nothing can be said.

Clever

When I grow up, I hope to be like me:
well-spoken, erudite and dignified,
the kind of man that one can wear with pride
and never overhear *you know that he*
is not at all what he pretends to be.
With proper bearing, it's a cinch to hide
the inside me inside the one outside
and work that trick with slick facility.

And when I master me I plan that I
inhabit who I am and where I've been—
then surreptitiously, conjoined, begin
to push and prod and nod, and clarify
a problem that we've never solved, but should:
is it better to be clever—or be good?

Rothko

black black black black black black
in tones of black and black on black
the canvases are tagged *abstract*
expressionist on every plaque
although the artist will attack
abstract and shun the word the lack
of it will not distract the claque
in black black black black black

brown brown brown brown brown
a message floats above the ground
serene reflective, and profound
a man who wound his own life down
red red red red red red red red
dead dead dead dead dead dead

About the Author

Michael Cantor's first full-length collection, *Life in the Second Circle* (Able Muse Press, 2012), was a finalist for the Able Muse Prize and 2013 Massachusetts Book Award for Poetry. A chapbook, *The Performer* (Pudding House Press) was published in 2007. His work has appeared in *The Dark Horse, Measure, Raintown Review, frogpond, New Walk, Think, Light,* and numerous other journals and anthologies. A native New Yorker, he has lived and worked in Japan, Latin America and Europe; and presently divides his time between Plum Island, MA, and Santa Fe, NM.

www.ingramcontent.com/pod-product-compliance
Lightning Source LLC
Chambersburg PA
CBHW022154080426
42734CB00006B/430